Helping Children See Jesus

ISBN: 978-1-64104-097-6

When I Am Weak
The Story of One of America's Founding Fathers

Author: Katie Zappitella
Computer Graphic Artist: Del Thompson
Page Layout: Patricia Pope

© 2020 Bible Visuals International
PO Box 153, Akron, PA 17501-0153
Phone: (717) 859-1131
www.biblevisuals.org

For a group-setting format of this story and other related items, please visit our web store at shop.biblevisuals.org and search using "5780".

On a bright, sunny Fourth of July, in the year 1791, the people of New Haven, Connecticut, were out in large crowds, excited to celebrate the 14th birthday of the United States of America. Rebecca Sherman peered out of her front door onto the bustling street, as she searched the crowds of happy holiday makers for her young grandson, Roger. Spotting him perched on the front fence, she called, "Roger! Time to come in for dinner!" The boy quickly jumped down from the fence and hurried inside where his grandfather was already seated at a large table. "Grandfather!" the boy exclaimed, "the people are speaking of you on the street! They look at the house as they go past and tell me that you are a great man and that our nation would not be as strong without you! What did you do, Grandfather? Did you defeat the whole British army? Are you a hero?"

The elderly Roger Sherman took off his spectacles and smiled down at his young namesake. "No, no, I am certainly not a hero. The good people of this city have exaggerated the story a bit. I was trained as a shoemaker, not as a soldier. Besides, I was too old to fight in the war for our independence. Despite all this, God has blessed me by allowing me to help with the founding of our nation in such ways as I am able. But," he chuckled softly, "I have certainly done nothing to earn the name of 'hero,' unless you count the ability to make a good, strong shoe."

"Listen to the man!" exclaimed Rebecca, bringing a dish of meat to the table, which was now full with children, grandchildren, and friends. "Now, Roger dear, your grandfather may not have been a soldier, but he is being far too humble. Let me tell you a few stories, and you will soon see why people love and respect him. Now, hush!" She laughed, stopping her husband, who looked ready to protest. "You sit quietly and eat, my love, but I want to tell my family the story of a great and godly man, and of a great God."

After Roger led a prayer of blessing for the meal, Rebecca continued her story. "Your grand-father was the second oldest in a family of seven children. After his father died, he had to leave school early to learn shoemaking and support his family. However, God had given him a passion for learning, and he was determined to learn all he could on his own. In fact, he would prop up books on his workbench and read in every spare moment he had! Even though he never finished school or went on to university, God blessed him as he taught himself. In fact, just recently Yale University gave him a college degree, saying he has learned enough to earn it even though he hasn't taken a single class!"

The children around the table looked up eagerly, the younger Roger asking, "Do you think I could do that? I would be very happy not to go to school!" Down the table Uncle Josiah, Grandfather's younger brother, stopped midbite and chuckled. "Although you may not always love school, children, it is a good thing, I promise! I used to feel the same way about school, especially after our father died. I wanted to leave school and care for my family. But even though your grandfather was only 19 when our father died, he worked hard to provide for us. In fact, although he would have loved to go to university, he worked and saved so that my brothers and I could go."

Roger looked up at his grandfather. "Wasn't that hard, Grandfather? Giving up something you wanted so much and letting someone else do it?"

Roger Sherman put down his fork and looked around the table for a moment before speaking thoughtfully. "Yes, it was a difficult time in my life. Losing my father was very hard and so was becoming responsible for my family at such a young age. But it was during this time that I truly learned to depend on the Lord for my strength. It is easy to think that we are strong, and that we can do anything we want to if we work hard enough. But we really can't!

Sometimes God brings us into hard times in order to show us how much we need Him. He loves us so very much and wants us to trust Him. During these years, God showed me my weaknesses and the greatness of Christ. I prayed that God would show me how I might serve Him—how to work hard, but also rely on Him, letting God lead me to do whatever He called me to do. God has richly answered that prayer!"

Rebecca passed around a plate of cookies, cut into stars like those on the first American flag, which she had helped her friend, Betsy Ross, sew. She then picked up her story. "I would say so! With the strength of God, your grandfather moved on from being a shoemaker to being all kinds of other things: a surveyor (a man who measures the land using math); a lawyer; a justice of the peace; a member of the government of Connecticut and the government of the United States; even the mayor of New Haven!"

Uncle Josiah cut in, "Ah yes, your grandfather was known for his abilities with math. In fact, he used to write almanacs, books which forecast the weather and the seasons and good times to plant and harvest, all using math and the stars in the nightime sky! One day, after one of his almanacs had been published, Roger was in the town courtroom working as the justice of the peace. Another man jokingly reminded him that his almanac called for rain even though the skies were clear. The men around him thought it was a great joke, and they all went off to lunch laughing.

But Roger was the only one to have a cloak that afternoon when, sure enough, it began to pour. That evening, your grandfather was the only man who came home dry!"

Amid the general laughter at this story, the elderly Roger smiled before adding, "Yes, God has blessed me in ways I never would have expected. But it wasn't always easy to trust Him. There were difficult times as well, especially when my dear first wife, Elizabeth, and two of our children died of illnesses. Through those dark times I struggled to remember that God loved me and that He was my strength. But," he remarked, looking at his wife with a twinkle in his eye, "little did I know the next blessing God had in store for me!"

Uncle Josiah grinned. "Roger came to visit me for a few days but was in a great hurry to leave and continue on to New Haven. I decided to ride with him for a short distance as he departed. While traveling down the road, who should appear riding toward us, but my wife's young niece, Rebecca, who was on her way to visit my wife.

"Naturally, I stopped to greet her, expecting to spend just a moment before carrying on with our journey. However, much to my surprise, Roger no longer seemed in a hurry. As a matter of fact, he insisted on turning our horses around and accompanying Rebecca back to my home." Uncle Josiah looked around at the children with a mischievous smile. "And do you know how long your grandfather, who had been in such a hurry to leave his dear brother, stayed?" Giggling, the children shook their heads. "He stayed for several more days! I'm quite sure it wasn't my wife's cooking or my good conversation that kept him there either. Although Rebecca was 22 years younger than your grandfather, it didn't take long for them to discover that they wanted to stay together for much longer. They were soon married."

Grandfather laughed and remarked, "Your grandmother is quite the woman! I would be most helpless without her advice and care. And she is a beautiful woman, too!"

"Did you know that one evening, when we were dining with many of our friends from Congress, George Washington himself escorted my wife into dinner, declaring that she was the prettiest lady in the room?"

Rebecca shook her head, half laughing, half vexed. "Oh, Roger, why do you tell the children such nonsense? Always remember, that handsome is as handsome does." "Well," replied her husband, "you looked handsome and acted handsome too, Rebecca; now it is my turn to praise you as a good example to our family." As the family enjoyed this story, playfully teasing Roger and Rebecca, young Roger took the opportunity to sneak another cookie or two from the plate before pulling his grandmother's sleeve. "But I still don't understand why the people in the street thought Grandfather was so important. How did he help our nation?"

"Goodness!" Rebecca replied. "I haven't even gotten to that part of the story, yet, and it is almost time to go to the town square for the Independence Day celebrations. Your grandfather was asked to help in the government very early, first here in Connecticut, and then with men from all the colonies. God has given him wisdom and thoughtfulness, and He put your grandfather in a place where he could use that wisdom to make good decisions for the colonies and eventually, for the United States of America.

As a matter of fact, your grandfather is the only man who helped to write and also signed all four documents that formed our nation: the Continental Association, the Declaration of Independence, the Articles of Confederation and the Constitution! *And* he was the one who had the wisdom to come up with a solution when states were arguing about how the government should be set up."

"That's right," said Uncle Josiah. "The big states wanted representation by population and the small states wanted representation to be equal for all states."

"What did you do, Grandfather?" asked young Roger.

Sherman smiled. "Well . . . I compromised."

"That's right," Rebecca added with a nod. "He suggested a government with two parts—one represented by population and one represented equally. Some people called it the Connecticut Compromise or Sherman's Compromise, but the smart ones call it the Great Compromise because it helped solve a big problem and brought the states into agreement to form the nation."

"Well, now," interrupted her husband, "while it is true that I was asked to help quite often, I truly needed God's strength. I was not comfortable speaking in front of people. Many of the men in Congress had gone to a university and had been taught how to speak well. Who was I, a poor shoemaker? What could I say or do? But God helped me to proclaim what I believed was right, even when I wasn't comfortable doing it.

"Do you remember, children, what God said to the apostle Paul? He said, *My grace is sufficient for you, for My power is made perfect in weakness.'* That's why Paul could say, *Therefore I will boast all the more gladly of my weaknesses, so that the power of Christ may rest upon me.*

"God has helped me to keep those words in my heart. He's taught me to be thankful for my weaknesses, because through them the power of Christ is shown clearly! I especially need to remember that as I prepare to speak in public, as I must do this afternoon."

A murmur of laughter went around the table as Rebecca exclaimed, "Ah, yes, your grandfather does not always make the most impressive figure when he speaks.

"He has always refused to wear a wig or dress in any finer clothing than the poor homemade things I sew. And he has such a way of standing, with one fist clenched at his side and the other clenched straight out before him! Although some men will laugh when they see him and hear the abrupt way in which he speaks, they soon stop when they hear what he has to say. Did you know," she added, looking around the table, "that Thomas Jefferson himself once said, 'That is Mr. Sherman of Connecticut, a man who never said a foolish thing in his life.'"

Uncle Josiah winked at his brother. "Well, I could probably give him an example or two!" The elderly Roger laughed. "I'm sure you could. Despite these words of praise, I know that I desperately need God each time I am given the responsibility of helping our nation. I am so easily tempted to trust in myself, or to seek to please people by saying and doing what they want me to. I have found great comfort and encouragement in reading God's Word. Every time I serve in Congress, I buy a new Bible to read and study during that session.

"At the end of the session, I bring that Bible home and give it to one of you. I want you all to know how important it is to continue reading God's Word and growing more like Him. Although I am now over 70 years old, I still need God every hour, whether resting on His strength, fighting against pride or struggling with my temper."

"Speaking of your temper, that reminds me of one more story! Then we need to leave or you will be late for your speech," Rebecca exclaimed. "I remember one day when I clearly saw that God was working in your grandfather's life. Roger continued to care for his mother, even after he had a home and family of his own. Every morning, Roger would lead devotions with our family and any friends or students who happened to be staying with us. One of the children was very small at the time and kept interrupting your grandfather. Finally he reached down and gently tapped her, more as a warning to behave. However, his mother saw the action and immediately stood up, hobbled over to Roger, and slapped him right across the mouth, exclaiming, 'You slap your child, I slap mine!' I remember holding my breath, wondering how Roger would respond. I could see the anger flash in his eyes. But, after a pause, he gained control over his temper and calmly went on with the devotion, without referring to the incident at all. That was God helping him to honor his mother and to respond with humility.

"But now, we must hurry and get ready!"

Rebecca jumped up from the table amid the laughter that resulted from this story and began directing the cleanup and the preparations to leave.

Roger turned to his grandson. "So," he concluded, resting his hand on the youngster's shoulder. "While I was involved in the founding of our nation, it was the hand of God that carried me through. Any gift I possess comes from Him. He helps me know what is true and right and gives me the courage to proclaim it. He alone deserves the glory and praise." The boy reached up and took his grandfather's hand. As they walked together out of the house, he responded thoughtfully, "Grandfather, I think I want to be like you when I grow up. I want to help our nation be strong and do what is right." Roger smiled. "I would love that, my son. But even more, I hope you grow up to love God and find your strength in Him, no matter where you serve Him."

And He said unto me, My grace is sufficient for thee: for My strength is made perfect in weakness. Most gladly therefore will I rather glory in my infirmities, that the power of Christ may rest upon me.

. . . for when I am weak, then am I strong.

2 Corinthians 12: 9, 10b

MAINE

NEW
HAMPSHIRE

MASSACHUSETTS

Boston

RHODE ISLAND

NEW
YORK

Providence

CONNECTICUT

New
Haven

PENNSYLVANIA

New
York

Wilmington

Philadelphia

NEW
JERSEY

Baltimore

DELEWARE

Annapolis

MARYLAND

VIRGINIA

Williamsburg

Norfolk

NORTH
CAROLINA

SOUTH
CAROLINA

Wilmington

GEORGIA

Charleston

Savanna

REVIEW QUESTIONS

1. What trade did Roger study as a young man? *(Shoemaking)*
2. Why did Roger have to leave school and help support his family? *(His father died when he was young.)*
3. How did Roger continue to learn, even though he had to leave school? *(He taught himself by reading while doing his work.)*
4. After his father died, who gave Roger strength for all he had to do? *(God)*
5. Name one of the jobs Roger was able to do. *(A surveyor, a lawyer, a justice of the peace, a member of the government of Connecticut and the government of the United States, the mayor of New Haven)*
6. What type of scientific books did Roger write? *(Almanacs)*
7. Who did Roger meet while visiting his brother, Josiah? *(Josiah's wife's niece, Rebecca, whom Roger later married)*
8. Who said Rebecca Sherman was the prettiest woman in the room? *(George Washington)*
9. Name one of the important documents Roger Sherman signed. *(The Continental Association, the Declaration of Independence, the Articles of Confederation and the Constitution)*
10. How did Roger help solve the problem of representation in government? *(He proposed a two-part system, one represented by population, one represented equally.)*
11. What was his solution called? *(The Great Compromise or The Connecticut Compromise or Sherman's Compromise)*
12. What are some weaknesses that God helped Roger overcome? *(His lack of education, his inability to speak well in public, his tendency to trust in himself or to please others, his temper)*
13. What did Roger look like when he spoke in public? *(No wig, homemade clothes, one fist clenched and the other clenched straight out in front of him)*
14. What book did Roger read while in Congress? *(The Bible)*
15. What did he do with the Bible after each session of Congress? *(He gave it to one of his children/grandchildren.)*
16. Who slapped Roger Sherman? *(His mother [Great-grandmother])*
17. Where does Roger say all our gifts and talents come from? *(God)*